Teachers' legal rights and responsibilities

A guide for trainee teachers
and those new to the profession

Teachers' legal rights and responsibilities

A guide for trainee teachers
and those new to the profession

Jon Berry

UNIVERSITY OF HERTFORDSHIRE PRESS

First published in Great Britain in 2007 by
University of Hertfordshire Press
Learning and Information Services
University of Hertfordshire
College Lane
Hatfield
Hertfordshire AL10 9AB

British Library Cataloguing in Publication Data
A catalogue record for this book is available from the British Library

ISBN 978-1-902806-77-8

Design by Geoff Green Book Design, CB24 5RA
Cover design by John Robertshaw, AL5 2JB
Printed in Great Britain by Cromwell Press Ltd, BA14 0XB

All advice in this guide pertains to the law as it affects schools in England and Wales only. Although there are occasions when legislation in these countries varies, nothing dealt with in these pages is affected by these differences.

Contents

Abbreviations

CRE	Commission for Racial Equality
DDA	Disability Discrimination Act
DfES	Department for Education and Skills
HEI	Higher Education Institution
IEP	Individual Education Plan
LEA	Local Education Authority
NQT	Newly Qualified Teacher
NUT	National Union of Teachers
OFSTED	Office for Standards in Education
QTS	Qualified Teacher Status
SEN	Special Educational Needs
SENCO	Special Educational Needs Co-ordinator

Acknowledgements

Cartoons by Tim Sanders: www.timonline.info

Many thanks to colleagues at the National Union of Teachers, particularly Graham Clayton and Amanda Brown, for their expertise and guidance. I'd also like to thank my predecessor in the writing of this guide, Nigel Gates, for his advice at the start of this project.

I'm hugely grateful to Ron Osborne, Tina Humber and Paul Holop, for allowing me to pick their brains about teachers' concerns and pre-occupations in this area and for their illuminating remarks, some of which are included here. Similarly, I'd like to acknowledge contributions from friends and colleagues along with my own student teachers.

The image of the 'Teacher' t-shirt at the beginning of the guide is reproduced by permission of Rosie Nieper: www.rosienieper.co.uk; 0870 2204455.

Foreword

I am delighted to have the opportunity to write this foreword. This guide to the extensive and detailed subject of education and the law will be of considerable interest to teachers, and to all those who are variously affected by its complexities and nuances. Jon Berry's experience both in the classroom and as a representative of teachers in a local education authority enables him to identify and explain effectively the legal framework within which teachers work.

Since moving into Higher Education, Jon has continued to demonstrate his commitment to meeting the needs of teachers in the classroom, as is evident in this guide. The guide promotes a better understanding of teachers' rights, duties, and responsibilities, which many teachers have neither the time nor the technical knowledge to glean from a direct reading of complex and jargon-ridden Regulations and Acts of Parliament.

Although the written word cannot be a substitute for expert and specialist advice and representation of the kind that the National Union of Teachers provides, I am sure that this guide will add significantly to the profession's understanding of a challenging but important subject.

Steve Sinnott
General Secretary
National Union of Teachers

What this guide sets out to do

The Welfare Worker lies awake,
But the law's as tricky as a ten-foot snake.

— 'Timothy Winters' by Charles Causley

Whether you are a teacher setting out on your professional career, or you've been teaching for some time, I hope that this guide will prove useful to you. There is no need for a teacher to be a legal expert, but every teacher should understand the basis of what the law requires in respect of education.

It is worth beginning with a word of caution – and a sense of perspective.

In their working lives, most teachers will have no serious brush with the law in regard to their professional duties. It is true that many of us will work in challenging circumstances and with difficult individuals, but that does not mean that even the most difficult situation will end up with you, as a teacher, facing legal action or prosecution. Such cases are extremely rare and should not colour the way in which we approach this subject. This sense of perspective is essential, and I shall be reinforcing it throughout the guide.

This guide will not answer all of your individual questions: no publication of this size could hope to cover every eventuality that besets teachers in their day-to-day work. What I hope to do is provide a clear working guide that will enable teachers to protect themselves in the most effective way possible, that is, to be forewarned and forearmed and so prevent difficult situations arising in the first place. (Needless to say, any teacher who embarks upon working with young people without having joined a trade union or professional association should not, in my view, think about leaving the house unaccompanied, never mind take charge of a class of any sort.)

The guide emphasises that teachers have rights as well as responsibilities. This may have become a rather unfashionable point to make, but just as the emphasis on rights could, in the view of some mid-range tabloid newspapers, have a potentially detrimental effect on how matters work, an over-emphasis on responsibilities without this balance can be equally harmful.

In this age of immediate access to information and documentation, I have not reproduced legislation in full except where it is useful to do so. Suggestions for further reading are included at the end of the guide, and the websites of teacher unions and other organisations listed there provide further and invaluable resources.

Professional duties

You may have seen this t-shirt, cheerily sported by some devoted teachers, the front of which lists a whole range of jobs from form filler to musician, accountant to pencil sharpener, and which finishes with the rather weary exhortation to 'just call me a Teacher!'.

Many teachers assume this mantle of utter dedication and commitment and are happy and proud to do so. On the other hand, you will come across plenty of grumpy old men and women who will be equally proud to tell you

Administrator, Social Worker,
Coat Finder, Arbitrator,
Government Directive Reader,
Curriculum Implementer,
Artistic Director, Form filler
Language Specialist, Pencil
Sharpener, Accountant,
Musician, Fundraiser, Report
Writer, Nose Wiper, Public
Relations officer, Petty Cash
Clerk, Examiner, Surrogate
Parent, Walking Encyclopaedia
Scapegoat . . . .
But you can just call me
a TEACHER!

that their job is just to teach the little so-and-sos, and at that point their professional commitment has been fulfilled.

Defining the extent of what teachers are expected to do, the range of their responsibilities, has been, to say the least, a tricky business for many years. During the industrial disputes of the 1980s, many teachers withdrew from activities which they regarded as coming under the umbrella of 'goodwill' and, as a reaction to this, the government of the time attempted to stipulate more exactly the hours and extent of teachers' duties. Despite the fact that this legislation, largely unaltered, still forms the basis of teachers' duties, there continues to be confusion, uncertainty, and a good deal of un-challenged folklore about what it is, precisely, that teachers have a legal obligation to know and do.

Although the exact wording of Qualified Teacher Status (QTS) standards may change from time to time, here are two basic points to remember.

Firstly, at the time of writing, the Standard relating to the attainment of QTS 1.8 states that teachers must 'be aware of, and work within, the statutory framework relating to teachers' responsibilities'. Although there may be slight changes to this phraseology over the years, it is difficult to imagine that this fundamental requirement will be altered in any way.

Secondly, it is worth knowing that all basic information relating to teachers' pay and their conditions of service can be found in the *School Teachers' Pay and Conditions Document*, which is published annually and is available online at www.teachernet.gov.uk. This is not exactly bedtime reading, but is still a fairly accessible document which clearly lays out teachers' obligations in terms of the hours and days when they must be available, cover, pay scales, and basic duties. Considering the fact that it contains so much information useful to teachers, it is slightly surprising that so few of us have read it, but it does provide a clear and authoritative reference point – and one that might well have proved useful to our t-shirt wearer, stipulating as it does that many of the routine administrative tasks undertaken by teachers in the past are now definitely precluded from their duties.

It goes without saying that the vast majority of teachers enter the profession with, at the very least, some sense of duty and service and, as a consequence, do not wish to see bureaucratic restrictions and petty rules dictate how they interact with the children in their charge. This is perfectly understandable and, indeed, even desirable. Few teachers count the hours or measure their commitment to school and pupils in the way that workers in some other trades and professions choose to do. Nevertheless, in ensuring that they fulfil their legal obligations and duties, it is equally important for teachers to be aware of how legislation also affords them protection and security: to be acquainted with such matters is not to be petty or confrontational, but is a way of ensuring that teachers' many responsibilities are balanced by their proper rights.

The duty of care to pupils

> A headmaster has introduced safety goggles for his pupils in a bid to stop the local council banning games of conkers in the playground. Shaun Halfpenny, the head of Cummersdale Primary School in Cumbria, feared the game would be banned after he read a council memo warning schools about dangerous break-time activities. It was suggested that youngsters could suffer eye injuries if struck by flying pieces of conker produced when the winner smashes the opponent's conker.
>
> – *Guardian*, 4 October 2004

One can only imagine the spluttering outrage, even of readers of liberal newspapers, when stories like the one above hit the headlines. Have we really reached the point where sensible individuals can consider banning robust games because of fear of freak accidents, or even the everyday bumps and scratches of childhood? Is this really what the concept of 'duty of care' has come to?

As we shall see in a moment, the answer is definitely not, but as a starting point – and without becoming too pedantic – it is worth considering what we mean by 'the law'.

Teachers' legal responsibilities derive from three sources:

* The common law duty of care (common law is the body of law derived from court decisions over the years as opposed to law which has been determined by Parliament and set down in statutes).
* The statutory duty of care arising from the *Children Act 1989*.
* The contractual duty of care as laid out in the *School Teachers' Pay and Conditions Document* (see above).

The common law duty of care

Ask most teachers what they understand by the application of duty of care and their response will almost certainly contain the phrase 'in loco parentis', in recognition of the fact that they are acting in place of a parent. This definition is only useful up to a point, stemming as it does from an 1893 court ruling that 'the schoolmaster is bound to take such care of his pupils as a careful father would'. Leaving aside the quaint gender bias of this ancient ruling, it is fairly obvious that such a judgement is fraught with potential difficulties of interpretation, not least of which is to consider whether 'a careful father' would, for example, allow his offspring to climb on PE equipment in the gym, peer over the edge of a muddy pond or, indeed, play conkers.

As a consequence, a more refined ruling in 1955 stated that 'a balance must be struck between the meticulous supervision of children every moment of the day and the desirable object of encouraging sturdy independence as they grow up'. It is this ruling which corresponds, of course, to the way in which most people would go about the business of supervising children, whether this be in the classroom or in the playground of their local park. By 1962 the courts had recognised that the 'standard of care' expected from a teacher was held to be that of a person exhibiting the responsible mental qualities of a *parent in the circumstances of a school, rather than home life.* The distinction is an important one, acknowledging as it does that the 'sturdy independence' of a child is to be encouraged, and that classroom activities may present the occasional risk.

What does this mean in real terms for the teacher preparing for an experiment in science, a nature walk, or a game of rugby? The critical thing to remember is that as long as a teacher has applied the ordinary skills of a competent professional, and that the teacher has acted in accordance with the views of a reputable body of opinion within their profession, the duty of care will have been met.

In an age where we can barely turn on the TV without seeing advertising claiming that huge sums of compensation are available for accidents and mishaps, it is hardly surprising that many teachers remain a bit jumpy about where they stand. Broadly speaking, however, individual teachers have little to fear just as long as they apply their professional judgement, experience, and training, and can demonstrate that their actions were taken with the best interests of the children in mind. The law will protect individual teachers in

Professional bodies

Most subject and curriculum areas have their own professional bodies that offer advice and information on a whole range of things. Only some of these are listed below.

The Association for Science Education
www.ase.org.uk

The Association for Physical Education
www.afpe.org.uk

The Geographical Association
www.geography.org.uk

RE Today (run by the charity Christian Education)
www.retoday.org.uk

The National Association of Advisers and Inspectors in Design and Technology
www.naaidt.org.uk

almost all cases – but cannot make allowances for any stupidity, negligence, or fecklessness on their part. Whether or not an individual teacher is found to be negligent will depend entirely upon whether an accident or mishap could reasonably have been foreseen; if teachers take reasonable (there's that word again) steps to ensure students' safety, the likelihood of their being found negligent is very slim indeed.

It is worth bearing in mind that in those rare cases where a teacher is found to be individually negligent, and where an injury occurs to a pupil as a consequence of this, compensation could be due to the child, this compensation being payable by the teacher's employer. The ramifications of this for any employee are obvious and could, of course, lead to disciplinary or capability proceedings for the teacher concerned (see p.44).

The final thing to consider in this section about the common law duty of care is collective or institutional failure or negligence, in which cases it is the school as an institution, rather than any particular individual, that is responsible for failing to execute its duties. This is most commonly manifested in the area of bullying, or as the result of dangerous or disruptive behaviour that goes unchallenged. In the event of a complaint from, for example, the victim of bullying, the extent to which the failure is collective or individual would be a matter that could be contested.

In summary: the law does *not* protect you if you have been stupid, lazy, or wilfully negligent, but if you have acted sensibly and in accordance with proper, professional procedures, you should have nothing to worry about.

The statutory duty of care

Teachers also have responsibilities under the *Children Act* 1989, which places duties upon those who care for children.

The *Children Act* represented a shift in legislation which brought to the fore a more child-focused approach to the law, asserting that the needs of the child are paramount. At the time of writing, schools and related agencies are working hard to incorporate the Every Child Matters agenda, which is one of the major developments arising from this shift. (See the section on 'Protecting children from abuse' on p.20, which discusses this initiative further.)

The Act declares that a person with care of a child may do all that is reasonable in the circumstances for the purposes of safeguarding or promoting the welfare of the child. As we shall see in later sections, this has ramifications for what a teacher may or may not do, especially in situations where a child is at risk of harm. Nevertheless, the main point of this part of the statute is to emphasise that the welfare of the child must be of prime importance when considering our duty of care.

The contractual duty of care

Although school life can present teachers and pupils with situations that may, on occasion, be potentially dangerous, the plain fact is that most children do not spend their school day abseiling down the Art block, mixing up Semtex, or tramping over Dartmoor without a compass. The majority of time on the majority of days is spent in perfectly safe classrooms engaged in perfectly safe activities. It is in these ordinary, everyday circumstances that teachers will fulfil the duty of care arising from their contract of employment, the terms of which have to comply with the *School Teachers' Pay and Conditions Document* (www.teachernet.gov.uk; this document should also be available at school).

The Document sets out clearly and unequivocally the terms of employment of all teachers. Matters such as contracted hours, the number of days you should be available for work, and the amount of cover you should do are properly outlined. Pay scales and the range of duties are also included. The Document is revised annually and takes effect in September of each year.

In precise terms this states that, unsurprisingly, teachers have to carry out their professional duties as circumstances may require under the reasonable direction of the head teacher of the school. In doing so, teachers are charged with promoting the general progress and wellbeing of individual pupils or of any class or group of pupils assigned to that teacher.

As well as these duties, teachers' duty of care extends to maintaining good order and discipline and safeguarding their pupils' health and safety, both when they are on school premises and engaged in authorised school activities elsewhere. Teachers are also contracted to attend assemblies (although there are exceptions allowing withdrawal on religious grounds) and register attendance.

All of the above should strike you, with good cause, as absolutely obvious. After all, that's what teachers do: teach, keep order, keep a general eye on the welfare, health, and safety of their pupils, and encourage them to fulfil their academic and personal potential. It cannot be emphasised too strongly that, in the everyday course of events, teachers who prepare lessons thoroughly, teach their classes with energy and enthusiasm, and mark and assess their pupils' work punctually and systematically will be fulfilling their common law, statutory and contractual duties of care to pupils to the letter.

Finally, a word about 'reasonableness'. Both in the execution of their own duties and in the definition of those duties by head teachers, the idea of reasonableness keeps reappearing. It goes without saying that lawyers grow fat on the debates arising from what is reasonable and what is not in any given set of circumstances; no legislation – let alone a guide of this sort – can allow for all eventualities. The test of what is reasonable is at the centre of many a wrangle, both in the courts and in your staffroom, and the very use of the term implies that there must be flexibility and a degree of broadness in its implementation. Deciding what is reasonable, particularly in difficult and fraught situations, is not always a clear-cut matter. However, what is critical at those times when disputes arise is that all parties enter into sensible dialogue with a view to speedy and effective resolution. For teachers this will almost certainly mean turning to your trade union or professional association for advice, and to leave yourself unprotected in this area is at best careless, and at worst, downright stupid.

Activities out of school

The school curriculum should … enable pupils to respond positively to opportunities, challenges and responsibilities, to manage risk and to cope with change and adversity.

– Aims for the School Curriculum, in National Curriculum, Department for Education and Skills (DfES), and Qualifications and Curriculum Authority, 1999

School trips are truly embedded in our curriculum. It would be a very sad day if we gave them up. Pupils learn a great deal about themselves and each other and experience an entirely different and beneficial sort of learning.

– Secondary school assistant head

For most people, school trips form some of the most enduring memories of their schooldays. As a pupil you may not have embarked upon them thinking that your education was being enhanced at every given moment: the stronger likelihood is that you spent at least a week beforehand sorting out the pecking order on the coach. Nevertheless, there is a clear and unchallenged understanding that such journeys, whether they involve a brief stroll around the local neighbourhood or a week's exchange in a school halfway across the globe, are of enormous educational, academic, and social value to pupils and staff alike. It is also encouraging that in a funded initiative announced in November 2006, aimed at prompting schools to reconsider their attitude to such activities, Education Minister Alan Johnson talks of how 'the law is there to protect [teachers] not inhibit them'.

It is regrettable, therefore, that the occasional, tragic mishap should have generated nervousness and unwillingness among a (very) few schools and teachers to embark upon such activities. This anxiety has, to a great extent, been reinforced by a perception that the paperwork involved in organising such events is so onerous as to be a deterrent in itself. These two elements are, of course, linked. As a reaction to the unfounded fear of an enormous lawsuit in the case of negligence, some schools do go about a belt-and-braces approach to risk assessment, which many teachers find both time-consuming and regard as unnecessary. Such an approach, as we shall see from the following paragraphs, largely arises from a misunderstanding of what is really necessary to demonstrate that proper duty of care has taken place. (On a purely practical note, it is also worth remembering that many schools now employ a non-teacher in the role of educational visit co-ordinator, or similar title, which removes the burden of this bureaucratic task from teachers.)

So how do individual teachers, as well as schools, protect themselves against legal liability? Let us start by reminding ourselves of two concepts with which, by now, we should be very familiar: negligence and reasonableness.

Unless it can be proven that an injury sustained by a pupil is as a direct result of *individual* negligence then a teacher is not liable.

There are a number of clear and obvious steps that any teacher can take in order to demonstrate that he or she is fulfilling their duty of care – and these steps need to be taken at the preparatory stage of a planned activity.

Vicarious liability

On the face of it, this rather grand sounding legal concept seems to be a 'get out of jail free' card for the individual teacher. What it means is that in case of accident or injury that could lead to legal liability, it is the employer – either the Local Education Authority (LEA) or the governing body, depending on the nature of the school involved – rather than the employee who is liable. This may sound all well and good for the individual teacher, but it is highly likely that any employer who is claimed against will pursue the teacher through the school's own disciplinary procedures should that employer believe the teacher involved has acted carelessly or imprudently.

Technically speaking, when it comes to voluntary activities out of school it would, indeed, be the teacher who is the named defendant in a case of potential negligence, which is why there is a longstanding agreement that employers have to obtain insurance cover for such activities, giving the same protection as if there were vicarious liability.

It is always worth remembering that there is no law or procedure in existence which will protect individuals who have acted without the due care and attention required in a given situation.

- Where it is relevant to do so, consult the advice given by relevant subject associations (some of which are listed on p.7)
- Read the advice given by the Department for Education and Skills (www.teachernet.gov.uk)
- Read any Local Education Authority advice available
- Read your school's policy, guidance, and advice

By taking the steps above, you should have a clear indication of such matters as the staffing ratio suggested, the level of risk assessment required, and the degree of supervision needed given the particular activity to be undertaken. By acting upon this advice, you will have gone a very long way to demonstrating that you have fulfilled much of your duty of care.

Sensible teachers know that the best way of dealing with any problem is to prevent it from actually arising in the first place. Much is the same with an out of school activity: if you feel that it has been inadequately prepared and organised and the level of preparation is *not* consistent with the advice given in the documentation above, then you should refuse to participate. Although the ultimate responsibility for any liability rests with your employer, it should go without saying that it is foolish to place yourself in a position where you believe that inadequate preparation has taken place.

So ... let us assume that all necessary preparation has been adequately completed: what about the situation once the activity is under way? Depending, of course, on the activity itself, the very point of many out of school events is to encourage the 'sturdy independence' of which the law speaks. How do teachers do this without either mollycoddling the pupils in their care, or setting themselves impossible tasks when it comes to adequate supervision?

Once again, it is important to go back to what is reasonable. The standard of care required from teachers is that which, from an objective point of view, can reasonably be expected from teachers generally applying skill and awareness of the problems, needs, and susceptibilities of children. The law expects the teacher to do what a caring parent would do whilst bearing in mind that taking responsibility for twenty pupils is entirely different from looking after a family. The legal duty of care expected of the individual is what a caring teaching profession would expect of itself.

In real terms what does this mean? Can a teacher, for example, allow a small group of Year 6 pupils to explore a particular exhibition in a museum unsupervised? Should a group of Year 10s visiting an exhibition or careers fair be set free in an unfamiliar city during their lunch break? At what time should a group of Year 12s be told to be back in their Paris hotel? Unsurprisingly, there are no clear-cut answers here and that is because, ultimately, any teacher has to apply professional judgement, consistent with each particular case whilst, most importantly, taking into account their knowledge and understanding of the abilities and capabilities of any given group of pupils. What is of paramount importance is that an individual teacher is confident that he or she has taken all reasonable steps to avoid exposing pupils to dangers which are foreseeable, and with which those pupils may not be expected to cope. It is critical that the level of risk is commensurate with what that teacher knows about the groups or individuals involved. It is a pretty trite thing to say, but not all twelve-year-olds are the same, and it is up to the teacher to make judgements in the light of this.

Supervisors

On certain trips and for certain activities, supervision of pupils will be handed over to specialist guides and instructors. Technically, pupils are still under the direct supervision of the teacher in these circumstances. It goes without saying, therefore, that the credentials and qualifications of such instructors need to have been thoroughly checked and verified – preferably, of course, before any such event has been planned. If you are in any way uncertain about the qualifications or expertise of such instructors, pupils should be withdrawn from the activity.

What of those pupils who refuse to obey instructions, or who disregard advice or important information? Fundamentally, the situation here is little different from that in the classroom. It is a rather foolish teacher who believes that an instruction given once in a classroom will immediately be acted upon by the entire class: points will need to be repeated and certain groups or individuals will need to be targeted for extra emphasis. Occasionally, different arrangements will need to be made for groups or individuals with particular needs, whether or not their inability to cope stems from wilfulness or lack of basic understanding. Much the same principles apply to out of school activities. Teachers need to take into account that some challenging or uncooperative behaviour may take place, and this needs to be seen in the context of the potential consequences of pupils disobeying rules and instructions. Balanced against this is the need to give pupils a degree of latitude consistent with what teachers know about their level of personal responsibility.

Given that practically all of this seems to be plain old common sense, you could be forgiven for asking yourself what all the fuss is about in relation to out of school activities. Don't misinterpret this: there is no doubt that for all their evident value, school trips are just as exhausting as they are rewarding for the average teacher! There is no suggestion that there is nothing to be learnt from the occasional tragic event, and many of us engaged in such activities can probably think of instances where we were moments from potential disaster. Nevertheless, as far as your legal responsibilities are concerned, these are the questions you need to ask yourself in order to ensure that you have fulfilled your legal obligations:

- Have I read and acted upon all of the relevant advice: subject association, DfES, LEA, school policy?
- Have the credentials and qualifications of any external supervisors been verified?
- Are the planned activities commensurate with what I know about the abilities and level of responsibility of the pupils involved?

Even experienced teachers will need to discuss some of these issues with colleagues before embarking upon such activities, and with teaching, as with everything else, there are no risk-free activities. However, careful and thorough preparation, along with a clear understanding of what 'duty of care' really means, will protect you when taking part in one of the best and most memorable elements of your teaching career.

Health and safety at work

With every week that passes, my list of pet hates grows longer. "Your call is important to us"; silicone implants; "thank you for not smoking"; ... cold callers; "celebrity" anything; health and safety ...
— Tom Utley, *Daily Telegraph,* 9 September 2005

Exactly how legislation introduced to ensure that workers can be suitably protected as they go about their day-to-day business has attracted such ranting opprobrium is something of a mystery. Nevertheless it has, unfortunately, become somewhat commonplace in certain circles to equate health and safety with petty and obstructive behaviour. Given that adherence to basic health and safety principles can be a matter of life and death, it is a shame that it often receives such an unfortunate and unjustified press.

The *Health and Safety at Work Act* 1974 is the principal piece of legislation dictating what is required in this important area of school life. It is critical to remember that prime responsibility under the Act rests with the employer rather than the employee. In the first instance this means that employers have to ensure that they have taken reasonable care for the health and safety of employees and others on their premises. Of course, this has implications for you as an employee: should you feel that such reasonable care is *not* being taken, it is a matter of *duty* for you to pursue this, either through a line manager or union representative. Failure to act on an issue that could result in injury to a pupil, where early intervention or reporting on a teacher's part may have prevented this, could in some circumstances point to individual negligence. As ever, in your relationship to the law as an employee, what is vitally important is that you act in a proper and professional way, following such advice as is available: by doing so, you will place responsibility firmly at the door of the employer where it properly rests.

Before we look at exactly who is responsible for what, let us pause for a moment and think about what health and safety issues mean in the daily context of school life. I have already made fleeting reference to what is currently called the 'compensation culture'. The comical manifestations of this are in the advertisements on TV, where some hapless soul recreates the fall or tumble that resulted in their acquisition of enormous riches. As crude as these adverts are, they do encapsulate a basic truth about health and safety: minor spillages, uncollected rubbish, faulty fittings, and unchecked appliances cause preventable accidents that can cause injury. To protect yourself under the law, it is your duty to report these apparently inconsequential matters to whoever is charged with dealing with them. In almost all schools there will be a recording system for accidents and you must familiarise yourself with this and use it in the proper way.

So, although basic responsibility does, indeed, rest with the employer, this does not exonerate the employee in any way whatsoever. The Act is entirely clear that all employees have to take care of the health and safety of themselves as well as others who may be affected by their acts or omissions at work. So, don't ...

- prop the door open with the fire extinguisher
- put the chair on the table and then stand on it so that you can just finish off that final bit of the display
- bring in your electrical extension lead from home to get the tape recorder in the correct position
- just dump that box of books by the fire door for five minutes

Sound familiar? (And just in case you detect a degree of smugness, I have been guilty on all counts.) Section 8 of the Act tells us clearly that it is unlawful to interfere with or misuse, either intentionally or recklessly, anything which has been provided for the purposes of health and safety. Moreover, the Act demands that teachers should act with reasonable care at all times and apply good sense to everything they do. It goes without saying that the examples above – and all of the other good-natured but slightly idiotic things that teachers do – do not fit into the category of 'good sense', and that by acting in such a way teachers potentially forfeit their protection under the law.

Balanced against this is the fundamental precept that employers have to organise, monitor, control, and review how health and safety measures are managed. They also have to assess risks and, most critically, inform their employees of procedures and policies; such policies should be in writing and easily accessible. It is the employee's responsibility to become familiar with these policies and procedures, and to act upon them accordingly.

It may sound fanciful to say that in the middle of preparing lessons, marking work, attending meetings, and just getting on with your life as a teacher, you should then find the time to locate and read such policies (especially in the whirlwind at the start of your career), but not to do so could be placing yourself in a difficult situation. A few moments spent reading a policy document could save a lot of time and trouble later on.

Protecting children from abuse

Legal responsibility for child protection rests with local authorities, schools, and colleges: schools have a legal duty to assist local authority social service departments acting on behalf of children in need or enquiring into allegations of child abuse. Once again, this legislation stems from the *Children Act 1989*, and is further supported by the *Education Act 2002*, which obliges schools and colleges of all sorts to have regard to the promotion of the welfare and safety of all children. As well as this, of course, the statutory duty of care discussed on p.8 places obligations on schools and teachers.

The phrase 'child protection' is a weighty one and its very mention is an indication that we are going into an area that is delicate and potentially disconcerting. In the light of this, it is worth carefully unpicking the structures and procedures that must be in place in every school as it is these, above all else, which form the foundation of how we approach this subject.

In every school there must be a member of staff with designated responsibilities for child protection. This individual is pivotal; and if you're reading this guide as a trainee, a Newly Qualified Teacher (NQT), or a relatively inexperienced member of staff, then it certainly shouldn't be you. However, it is your responsibility to ensure that you can identify who this person is in your school. It is the job of this designated individual to ensure the application of local, regulatory, and statutory requirements, in order that all legal obligations in this area are met.

Under no circumstances should you, personally, make any attempt to investigate any suspicions you may have about potential abuse. Any such suspicions must be reported to the designated member of staff, using the agreed procedures within the school. Furthermore, once you have reported any suspicions in the agreed manner, you should not pursue the matter in any way unless specifically directed to do so by the designated teacher: to do

Every Child Matters

Anyone now working in schools will soon be made aware of this government initiative. The five outcomes of the scheme are that we should all work to ensure that children should:

- Be healthy
- Stay safe
- Enjoy and achieve
- Make a positive contribution
- Achieve economic wellbeing

The website for this initiative, www.everychildmatters.gov.uk, gives this description of the project:

> This means that the organisations involved with providing services to children – from hospitals and schools, to police and voluntary groups – will be teaming up in new ways, sharing information and working together, to protect children and young people from harm and help them achieve what they want in life. Children and young people will have far more say about issues that affect them as individuals and collectively.

For teachers this most definitely does *not* mean that we all have to become everything from a social worker to an economic adviser, but it does mean that we have to recognise that schools are expected to work as an integral part of a multi-agency approach to the wellbeing of children. However, the major implementation of the scheme will be addressed at a senior level in the school, with, once again, the designated lead professionals being the most important individuals in the process.

so could be potentially damaging to all parties, including you.

In terms of detection of abuse, some signs such as physical manifestations or changes of behaviour on the part of the pupils may be reasonably obvious. On occasion a pupil may write something or produce a piece of work that may give you cause for alarm: in the event of this causing such concern, it is your legal duty to report it in the appropriate way. It is also sometimes in the nature of the job that a pupil may confide in you, asking you to keep a matter confidential. It is critical for you to understand that you cannot undertake to maintain such confidentiality should a child ask you to do so, and you must make that entirely plain to the child in question.

Until such time as you choose to be the designated member of staff with responsibility for child protection, you will have fulfilled your duty of care by acquainting yourself with the procedures, key personnel, and policies within your particular school, and then acting accordingly.

But what about the real nightmare ...

... of the accusation against you?

In the few months prior to writing this guide I watched two major TV dramas in which the central plot was based on a malicious allegation against a teacher. (One can only begin to imagine the astonishment with which, for example, police officers and medical staff must watch the plethora of such programmes about their own professions.) Fantastic drama – and both programmes were pretty good – doesn't always sit that easily with the rather humdrum and mundane procedures which, inevitably, accompany such dreadful events. So, in keeping with the sense of perspective that I have tried to maintain throughout this guide, let us just look at the extent of the problem.

In a 2006 survey, the National Association of Schoolmasters Union of Women Teachers found that of some 1,800 allegations made against teachers, only 69 (around 3 per cent) had even a degree of credibility. In a House of Commons reply in December 2004, the then Minister for School Standards, David Miliband, revealed that only 17 per cent of such cases ended in prosecution. Put another way, the number of allegations against teachers ending in prosecution is statistically insignificant. Which is fine, just as long as you're not the one who is accused.

There is little doubt that being such a victim is traumatic in the extreme, and it is in such cases that the whole idea of the law affording teachers rights as well as responsibilities comes into play. Later on, we'll be looking in a little more detail at what happens should you fall foul of general disciplinary and capability matters, but in the rare event of your being the victim of a malicious allegation, there are a few things that it is vital to remember.

The first of these is to contact your trade union or professional association without delay. (It is worth bearing in mind that most such organisations will *not* permit you to join retrospectively; especially, of course, as such cases could be protracted and use a great deal of time and expertise.) Secondly, you must be furnished with a copy of the procedures under which the school is acting and, obviously, you will need to read these and ask questions of your union official. Thirdly, say and do absolutely nothing until advised to do so: although it may be difficult, you need to adopt the attitude of the hard-faced criminals of TV drama who stay entirely mute until their brief arrives.

There is, regrettably, little to lighten such incidents. Police and social services may be mentioned and could even become involved, and that, in itself, is worrying and unnerving for anyone. However, a highly developed, well-refined, and thorough system means that the stuff of teachers' nightmares rarely becomes reality. A great deal of public debate in recent years has led many people to believe that the rights of accusers outweigh those of the accused in such situations: fortunately, statistics and facts belie that belief. Nonetheless, as with so much of what we've already covered, the trick is to be forewarned and forearmed. The law protects you, the teacher, as much as it does children, and the best thing you can do is to make sure that you are aware of agreed procedures and practices in your school, thereby ensuring that the chances of your being liable remain extremely slim.

Physical contact with pupils

When talking to some trainee teachers about this topic recently, the conversation started with a primary teacher telling the group about a child who regularly and systematically came into school in the morning, dumped her bag and coat wherever (in)convenient and came up to give her a cuddle. What, this new teacher wanted to know, was she supposed to do about that? Her concern and slight discomfort stem from one of the most popular misconceptions to have dogged the profession in recent years: teachers, apparently, are not to touch pupils under any circumstances. It is, of course, not difficult to see where this misunderstanding may have come from – and it is critically important that teachers understand the legal and professional parameters within which they have to work when it comes to touching pupils – but it certainly is a misunderstanding and one that needs careful unpicking.

Having reached this point in the guide, a number of phrases and principles should now be familiar to you. Of these principles the one that dictates that you should be completely conversant with school policy and practice, with the direction of the head teacher, is paramount. It is just about possible that the head teacher of the school in question had issued a directive that staff must not touch, cuddle, or comfort children in any way; if that were the case it would be foolish for any member of staff to disregard that advice. What is more likely, however, is that the head would have issued advice similar to that which appears in various DfES circulars and advisory documents.

It is worth quoting Circular 10/98, which deals with the use of physical restraint, at some length:

There may be occasions where a distressed pupil needs comfort and reassurance which may include physical comforting such as a caring parent would give. Staff should use their discretion in such cases to ensure that what is normal and natural does not become unnecessary and unjustified contact, particularly with the same pupil over a period of time. Where a member of staff has particular concern about the need to provide this type of care and reassurance they should seek the advice of the head teacher.

Some staff are likely to come into physical contact with pupils from time to time in the course of their duties. Staff should be aware of the limits within which such contact should properly take place and of the possibility of such contact being misinterpreted.

As one primary deputy head says, 'Be careful. Keep it minimal – a pat on the back at the very most.'

The *TeacherNet* website amplifies this advice:

Physical contact may be misconstrued by a pupil, parent or observer. Touching pupils, including well-intentioned gestures such as putting a hand on the shoulder can, if repeated regularly, lead to serious questions being raised. As a general principle, staff must not make gratuitous physical contact with their pupils. It is particularly unwise to attribute touching to their teaching style or as a way of relating to pupils.

This advice is a long way from a simple 'don't touch' directive, but it is plain to see that it is hedged around with a number of caveats, most of which are blindingly obvious. We're back, once again, to the idea of a caring parent in the circumstances of the school, adherence to policies and advice, and the application of a degree of common sense.

There are also, of course, any number of other occasions where touching, supporting, and physically guiding pupils are intrinsic parts of the actual teaching process. It is at this point that subject associations come into play. The following advice, for example, from the website of the Child Protection in Sport Unit, gives a flavour of the sort of specific advice that is available:

Physical contact during sport should always be intended to meet the child's needs, NOT the adult's. The adult should only use physical contact if their aim is to:

- Develop sports skills or techniques

Ladies and gentlemen of the class of '97 ... wear sunscreen.
If I could offer you only one tip for the future, sunscreen would be
IT.

         – Mary Schmich, *Chicago Tribune, Wear Sunscreen*

Council chiefs say they have had no complaints from parents over claims some children in Denbighshire would be kept indoors unless they apply their own sun cream. Vale of Clwyd Assembly Member Ann Jones said one parent had protested to her that her child's school had issued the warning. The council said individual schools and parents should decide whether teachers put cream on young children in the sun.

         – *BBC News* website, 7 June 2006

The story of the teachers banned from applying sun cream falls, of course, into the 'world gone mad' category so beloved by parts of the media. The position would have been clearer, however, if only things had happened in a perfect world. The schools could, and perhaps should, have alerted parents to the need to supply children with sun cream for outdoor activities during periods of hot weather. Such a communication would also have alerted parents to the fact that, should teachers be concerned that cream had not been applied adequately or correctly – and how many excited six-year-olds might be trusted to have done so? – then they would intervene and do so unless otherwise instructed by the parent or carer. Duty of care would then have been fulfilled, and the needs of the child, as well as concerns over health and safety, would have been catered for. It goes without saying, nonetheless, that any sensible and thoughtful teacher would wish to apply sun cream to a child in the presence of another adult.

- To treat an injury
- To prevent an injury
- To meet the requirements of the sport

The adult should explain the reason for the physical contact to the child. Unless the situation is an emergency, the adult should ask the child for permission.

As one primary teacher commented, 'Even with very young kids I always say, "Can I show you?"'

In another example, the online journal of Music Teachers UK directs its readers to the website of the Musicians' Union, which gives the following advice:

> Most instrumental teachers may find themselves in situations where they are likely to come into physical contact with their pupils in the course of their duties. All instrumental teachers should be aware of the context in which such contact should properly take place and of the possibility of such contact being misinterpreted. Instrumental teachers working with individual or small groups of pupils are potentially subject to a much greater threat of misinterpretation of such actions, or indeed of malicious allegations. The best advice at all times is for instrumental teachers to avoid physical contact with pupils except when absolutely necessary, and then to ask another adult to be present to observe their actions.

There will be similar examples from all subject associations across the curriculum. The point about this is that as long as teachers comply with the advice given locally (by their school and/or local authority) along with that of a reputable public body (recognised associations, trade unions), those teachers will have gone about their business properly, and will have fulfilled their duties and obligations to the letter.

None of this, however, condones physical punishment in any way whatsoever. The law here is unequivocal, emphasising that both physical punishment and physical responses to misbehaviour are unacceptable unless they are by way of restraint (which we will deal with in the next section).

Finally, on the topic of touching, there are of course many teachers working in special circumstances with children with specialised and complex needs, and for whom the guidance applicable to mainstream schools will often be inadequate. Such teachers will be given particular guidance and training, and can also find documentation in the DfES Circular LEA 0242, which addresses this specialist area.

Physical restraint

Sometimes the advice from central government, clear and well intentioned as it is, can sound just a touch comical and strait-laced in its use of understatement. DfES Circular 10/98 advises us that, 'Before intervening physically a teacher should, wherever practicable, tell the pupil who is misbehaving to stop, and what will happen if he or she does not'.

The advice, difficult as it may be to follow, is sound and sensible, and we'd all like to think that we'd be able to follow it. The passage goes on to say that:

> The teacher should continue attempting to communicate with the pupil throughout the incident, and should make it clear that physical contact or restraint will stop as soon as it ceases to be necessary. A calm and measured approach to a situation is needed and teachers should never give the impression that they have lost their temper, or are acting out of anger or frustration, or to punish the pupil.

The 'calm and measured approach' of which the Circular speaks might not be the easiest thing to maintain in a situation that, by its very nature, could be tense and fraught. Nevertheless, knowing where you stand, what you are entitled to do, and what is expected of you, should go some way to helping you deal with the situation. (Again, it is worth a reminder that such incidents are not daily occurrences.)

Most of the current legislation about restraint stems originally from Section 550A of the *Education Act 1996*, now largely superseded by Sections 88–93 of the *Education and Inspection Act 2006*, which is summarised in the Circular mentioned above. Once again, it is useful to look at the actual wording of the Circular:

Teachers, and other persons who are authorised by the head teacher to have control or charge of pupils, [may] use such force as is reasonable in all the circumstances to prevent a pupil from doing, or continuing to do, any of the following:

- Committing a criminal offence (including behaving in a way that would be an offence if the pupil were not under the age of criminal responsibility)
- Injuring themselves or others
- Causing damage to property (including the pupil's own property)
- Engaging in any behaviour prejudicial to maintaining good order and discipline at the school or among any of its pupils, whether that behaviour occurs in a classroom during a teaching session or elsewhere

The first thing that our practised eye should immediately notice is the phrase 'authorised by the head teacher'. As a teacher in a school, you have to assume that, under your contractual obligations, you are such an authorised person. It should also be noted that this obligation falls upon you not just on school premises, but anywhere else where you have lawful control of any pupils, such as an outing or a trip.

For all of the above, my strong suspicion is that the main concern of the majority of teachers would be: 'What if I, personally, do not feel capable of exercising physical restraint or do not have the confidence, in a given situation, to do so?' In these circumstances the law protects teachers as well as placing obligations on them. If, for example, the incident involves a large pupil – or more than one pupil – or if the teacher believes that she or he may be at risk of injury, then other pupils who may be at risk should be removed, assistance summoned from a colleague and, until such assistance arrives, the teacher should attempt to defuse the situation orally and try to prevent the incident from escalating. Obviously, doing nothing and waiting for situations to fizzle out is simply not an option, and such an unwise approach is not only negligent in general terms but, more significantly, in legal ones as well.

You would never enter a situation requiring physical restraint unless you knew you could definitely cope with the situation.

– Secondary school assistant head

The next tricky area is one where no law can be comprehensive or definitive.

Once a teacher has made a decision to intervene physically, potential problems lie in the precise nature of that intervention. The terms of the Act as described in the DfES Circular are useful up to a point:

> The use of force can be regarded as reasonable only if the circumstances of the particular incident warrant it. The use of any degree of force is unlawful if the particular circumstances do not warrant the use of physical force. Therefore physical force could not be justified to prevent a pupil from committing a trivial misdemeanour, or in a situation that clearly could be resolved without force.
>
> The degree of force employed must be in proportion to the circumstances of the incident and the seriousness of the behaviour or the consequences it is intended to prevent. Any force used should always be the minimum needed to achieve the desired result.

Clearly, the law cannot unequivocally prescribe exactly what is required in every situation. The age and strength of the children involved are principal determinants as, of course, is the degree of risk or danger arising from a particular event. We have spoken before of reasonableness, and this concept comes into play here, as well as that of proportionality. We have to hope that we can get through our careers without having to use any form of physical restraint – and we've already touched on the concept of what is reasonable

If absolutely necessary you may consider:	But don't even think about:
Physically interposing yourself between pupils	Holding around the neck or restricting breathing
Holding	Slapping, punching, or kicking
Pushing	Twisting or forcing limbs
Leading by the hand or arm	Tripping
Shepherding by placing a hand in the centre of the back	Holding by the hair or ear (older colleagues may remember this as being practically compulsory for some teachers)
Using restrictive holds in extreme circumstances	Holding a pupil face down on the ground

and what is not – but if the worst comes to the worst, the law does then give us some clear 'dos and don'ts'.

The potentially acceptable measures listed above may also be used in a preventative way in order, for example, to stop a child from running onto a road or from throwing something.

Teachers should always avoid touching or restraining pupils in any way that may be considered indecent.

To reiterate an earlier point, in the heat of the moment it may not be possible to make finely nuanced judgements, but knowing beforehand that our actions must be informed by the immovable principles of safety, responsibility, and reasonableness should help to extricate ourselves from difficulty, as well as protecting against claims of negligence.

All serving teachers, at whatever stage in their career, should ensure that they have been given the correct information and procedures relating to their particular school. As always, the law will protect where it can, but ignorance and omission are not defences against accusations of negligence.

Discipline

There is a general perception that school discipline is out of control. While there is clearly a problem in a minority of schools, most children behave well, most of the time.

– Website of the Department for Education and Skills

I read in the paper of American school teachers' problems with unruly adolescents who have never been disciplined.

– *The Diary of Nellie Last*, 15 January 1943

As a trainee teacher, I don't see how a government can improve behaviour in the classroom in the short term. Surely it is society at large, and not just education policy that is at fault here ...

– View expressed on the website of the BBC

A teaching colleague of mine once claimed that when asked about his job at parties he would say he was a cobbler, on the grounds that he was fairly certain this was an occupation about which his fellow guests would not have an instant – and probably ill-informed – viewpoint. Whether or not his strategy was effective – or, indeed, whether or not it was even true (I never actually saw it in action) – it is an illuminating anecdote. Everyone has a view about teaching, and *absolutely* everyone has a view about discipline or behaviour management in schools.

Broadly speaking, the consensus is that there has been a gradual deterioration over the years, and that the rigours of 'good old-fashioned discipline' are a thing of the past. TV shows like *Bad Lads' Army* and *That'll Teach 'Em*, not to mention *Grumpy Old Men* and *Grumpy Old Women*, have helped to reinforce this viewpoint. There is, of course, no way of making sensible, informed comparisons between generations on this subject, but there is no escaping the fact that the behaviour of pupils remains one of the main – if not the main – preoccupation of almost all teachers. Given this, and given that on the issue of classroom control he or she who hesitates is most definitely lost, it is vitally important for teachers to know where they stand as far as the law is concerned.

Firstly, and notwithstanding the mythology of the effective 'clip round the ear' which served previous generations, any form of touching, restraint, or force used as a disciplinary measure is entirely unacceptable in any circumstances. There are no exceptions to this, and any teacher who uses such measures will not be protected by the law.

All schools will have a system of procedures for behaviour management: although broadly similar, there may be differences of emphasis and style. The most recent piece of relevant legislation, the *Education and Inspection Act 2006*, is unequivocal in its position with regard to the right of teachers to discipline pupils, and the support they should receive, with the White Paper from which it stemmed declaring that:

> We will introduce a clear and unambiguous legal right for teachers to discipline pupils, backed by an expectation that every school has a clear set of rules and sanctions ... we believe that the right to discipline should be set down clearly in law so that no parent can again question a teacher's authority on this matter, when he or she is acting reasonably.

Teachers new to the profession may well regard a school's system as one of the principal reasons for choosing to work there, or not. What is important to appreciate is that whatever system a school chooses to employ, that's the one you will have to implement in your day-to-day conduct. Going back to the idea of our contractual duties, this system will be the directive of the head teacher, and putting it into practice will go a long way to protecting yourself in a legal sense. On those occasions where teachers find themselves in difficulty in the area of behaviour management, it is often because agreed school procedures have not been followed, and a teacher has made up some ad hoc punishment on the spot and in the heat of the moment.

Perhaps the most contentious area of debate when it comes to the punishment of pupils is that of detention. When that impertinent thirteen-year-old gleefully tells you that you can't put her in detention because you ain't given her twenty-four hours of notice, is she correct? And how long should it be for? And what should pupils be doing in that time? Although most school policies worth their salt will deal with these issues, the law, through Section 550B of the *Education Act 1996*, is helpful and illuminating.

Perhaps the most surprising thing for most teachers to know is that the law allows for the detention of pupils at the end of school sessions (and this, of course, need not necessarily mean the end of the day itself) *without parental consent*. However, for detention to be put into practice, certain preconditions have to apply.

The first of these is that it must be generally known that the detention of pupils is part of the school's disciplinary system. This must have been made clear to parents and pupils beforehand through whichever means a school chooses to employ, such as newsletters, parents' meetings, or information on websites. The critical thing is that everyone must know detention is a sanction used in that particular school.

Secondly, the law is clear that the detention 'must be reasonable in all the circumstances'. Consideration should be taken in relation to age and ability as well as any special needs that pupils may have. Travel arrangements may be a further concern, as well as any religious or cultural issues that may be significant. Any punishment, including tasks set as punishment during the detention, needs to be proportionate.

For example, many schools choose not to implement after-school detentions during the winter months when travelling home alone and after dark may be an issue; especially, perhaps, for girls. In these circumstances, should a school choose to use detention as part of its system and should it want such detentions to take place at another time of the day, then as long as this arrangement has been made clear to parents and pupils, it is legitimate to act in this way.

However, do note that teachers' contractual duties as laid out in the *School*

Keeping them back for five minutes

Very often, classroom situations arise in which a teacher wants to make a point about lateness, minor disruption, or mildly irritating behaviour from a class or an individual and, as a consequence, will threaten to prevent a class from going to break or lunch. It's nothing like a full-blown detention, but it is a response to an immediate situation that a short, sharp reprimand may resolve. Is this legitimate? Is it a 'detention'?

The answer, as always, lies in the expectations of the school and what is contained in its policies. The law has nothing to say about these impromptu punishments, but the person waiting for their next lesson may well have! Check whether this is part of the school's way of operating before using this approach.

Teachers' Pay and Conditions Document also allow for 'a break of reasonable length between school sessions' and so the supervision of such detentions may be an issue in some schools.

Twenty-four hours' notice of detention must be given to parents by whatever means a school has chosen to use. This could be by post, 'pupil post', email, or, increasingly commonly, by text message. However, the *Education and Inspection Act 2006* states that such notice is not required for lunchtime detentions.

As with all matters relating to behaviour management, the ultimate responsibility lies with the head teacher. When an individual teacher detains pupils, that teacher is doing so as the person authorised to do so; acting, in other words, as the head teacher's delegate. This is yet another instance where there is no substitute for knowing precisely what is expected from you in accordance with your own school's policies and procedures.

In this section about behaviour management there has been no attempt to delve into the whole area of suspensions and exclusions. For those at the start of their careers such momentous decisions are a long way off. For general information, you can acquaint yourself by reading through the material in DfES Circular 10/99 and it is definitely worth knowing your school's attitude to, and use of, such measures. However, it would be foolish in the extreme to use the threat of such measures as part of your approach to classroom management and general discipline.

Anti-discrimination and human rights

Low expectations of pupils by teachers often seem based on a stereotypical view that White/Caribbean (mixed heritage) pupils have fragmented home backgrounds and 'confused' identities. These pupils often experience racism from teachers and from their White and Black peers targeted at their mixed heritage.

– Research from Drs Tikly, Caballero, Haynes and Hill,
Bristol University

Racism is still a reality in the life of some minority ethnic student teachers/trainees. HEIs [Higher Education Institutions] and partnership schools have an equal opportunities policy, but not a separate antiracism policy.

– *Multiverse* website, which provides teacher educators and student teachers/trainees with a comprehensive range of resources focusing on the educational achievement of pupils from diverse backgrounds

It is not necessary to prove that the other person intended to discriminate against you: you only have to show that you received less favourable treatment as a result of what they did.

– Advice from the Commission for Racial Equality (CRE)

The law prohibits discrimination on the grounds of sex, race and disability and, at the very time of writing this guide, legislation has been introduced to include the additional category of age. The law governing these areas is encompassed in the following Acts:

- The *Sex Discrimination Act 1975*
- The *Race Relations Act 1976* as amended in 2000
- The *Disability Discrimination Act 1995* as amended in 2001
- The *Human Rights Act 1998*
- The *Employment Equality (Age) Regulations 2006*

The idea that, as you gear yourself up to do battle with your rowdy Year 10s or to juggle the various needs of your mixed Year 5s, you ought to bear in mind the requirements of the *Human Rights Act 1998* may seem just a tad unrealistic. All the same, the fact that this slim but weighty piece of legislation does, indeed, apply to schools, along with the others listed above, gives an indication that we have to treat these matters with great seriousness.

We should start by saying that in the last three decades or so, most schools have been in the forefront of the battle against discrimination of all sorts. No one in their right mind would pretend that the situation is perfect, and the comment about the experience of trainee teachers at the start of this section is alarming and depressing. However, most schools do have anti-discrimination policies and these are reinforced by practice in and around what happens in classes. It is also true to say that the implementation and monitoring of these policies within schools will fall, in most cases, to senior managers and experienced teachers: for the time being, we will limit ourselves to looking at what a new entrant to the profession needs to know.

Let us start by making the clear and unequivocal statement that it is unlawful to discriminate against a pupil on the grounds of sex, race, colour, nationality, ethnicity, or national origins. Similarly, it is unlawful to discriminate on the grounds of sexual orientation, religion, or belief, and transgender issues also fall within the remit of sex discrimination. These principles are clear-cut and non-contestable.

Most, if not all, teachers would be horrified at the idea of discriminating against any pupils in such a way. However, the law about discrimination is not as straightforward as we might like it to be. Although there are obvious forms of discrimination such as abusive comments, others are not as immediately apparent. The low expectations referred to above, along with such things as subtle differences in assessment and provision, can be construed as discrimination – albeit that these things can be unwittingly done, and sometimes with the best of intentions. How might this happen?

It is at this point that we hit the most difficult and by far the most contentious area when it comes to discriminatory behaviour. For while there are few of us who would expend too much sympathy on the teacher who makes racist or sexist jibes, it does become trickier to unpick whether or not our actions have had the *effect* of being discriminatory, although we had not intended them to be so. The legal concept of indirect discrimination is described in the CRE quotation at the start of this section: irrespective of whether there is *intent* to discriminate, it is the *outcome* that is important.

What does this mean in our classrooms? A good place to begin is to look at the issue of cultural bias in questions used to assess students' abilities. This debate about cultural bias has raged in the educational world for decades and is best illustrated by looking at the old Eleven Plus exam, which was used to determine what sort of secondary schools pupils would attend. A significant part of the examination was based on IQ tests, in themselves a theatre of war for academics and educationalists. Questions would, for example, show incomplete pictures of a tennis court or a house and ask what was missing. The required answers would be, respectively, the net and the chimney, but it's not difficult to see the cultural specificity of such questions. This is, of course, a pretty crude and largely outdated example, but it is relatively easy to see how this exemplifies what we mean by cultural bias. Contemporary materials used in our classrooms have been produced and designed by teachers to avoid such obvious pitfalls, but vigilance is required to avoid falling into the trap of indirect discrimination.

On a broader scale – one which will probably not impact on the lives of newly qualified or inexperienced teachers – we can examine how a school, as an institution, can be guilty of indirect discrimination. In a case heard by the House of Lords, a school's insistence that all boys wear a cap as part of the school uniform was clearly discriminatory against Sikhs and was deemed to be unjustifiable on educational grounds. Beyond this, a school needs to ensure that its admission and application policies do not fall foul of the law, as well as ensuring that its exclusion rates do not demonstrate significant bias.

With regard to the issue of disability, the *Disability Discrimination Act 1995* (DDA) was amended in 2001 to include the education sector, making it unlawful to discriminate against disabled pupils and prospective pupils. It is fairly obvious that in a situation where not all schools are equipped to deal with all pupils with disabilities, the responsibility for overall provision of access lies with local authorities; but within schools themselves, the same approach to equality of opportunity in relation to sex or race applies to disability.

But it's not a problem in our school...

In his introduction to the 2004 DfES publication *Aiming High: Understanding the Educational Needs of Minority Ethnic Pupils in Mainly White Schools*, the Parliamentary Under Secretary of State for Schools, Stephen Twigg, wrote:

> Our aim is to help the schools in mainly white areas to create an environment where all pupils have access to a curriculum which embraces the range of cultural backgrounds across the country, where all teachers are aware of the needs of a particular group of pupils, and where the school workforce is equipped to meet the needs of a diverse learning community.

It might be very easy to think there is 'no problem' in your particular school, but to adopt such an attitude is to invite accusations of indirect discrimination as well as being in dereliction of your professional duty of care. Racist attitudes, if unchallenged, can be allowed to harden and become 'acceptable' in such an environment. The same goes for attitudes to disability and, in single sex schools, uncontested remarks of an offensive or prejudicial nature about the opposite sex.

The Sex Discrimination and Race Relations Acts work in tandem to ensure that all forms of prejudice are eliminated from our schools, but the legislation does more than just place a duty upon schools to prohibit discrimination. It emphasises the obligation to promote race equality and equality of opportunity. Hence, an attitude of 'no problem here' simply will not wash.

All staff and students at this school know that they benefit from having children with all sorts of needs and disabilities: we learn something new about each other all the time.

– Secondary school head teacher

As usual, we need to look at what all of this means for you: the teacher at the start of a career. And, once again, it comes down to being acquainted with the policies and practices of your particular school, which should, if properly formulated and effectively applied, work towards the elimination of discrimination and prejudice where you work.

It would be extremely naïve to think that schools are completely free of such discrimination. Regrettably, we sometimes become acutely aware of the fact that racist and sexist attitudes are far from rare in our classrooms, school corridors, and, yes, our staffrooms. It may also be extremely difficult for you as a new and relatively inexperienced member of staff to raise such concerns in a public way, and it is likely that you will need to consider which line manager or senior member of staff to approach about the existence of discriminatory behaviour. Later on in this guide we shall deal with exactly what you are able to do when policies, however laudable, are bypassed and ignored. In the meantime, two principles should underlie your actions. Firstly, ensure that your own professional practice is non-discriminatory in every aspect of what you do. Secondly, consult your trade union or professional association when you have anxieties in this area: if that body is not vigorous when addressing matters of discrimination, change and join one that is immediately.

Finally, remember that laws proscribing discrimination protect you, the teacher, as well as the pupil. In terms of recruitment, promotion, and access to benefits and services, it is illegal for employers to discriminate on the grounds of race, sex, marital status, sexual orientation, religion or belief, disability, transgender status, trade union membership or activity, or by reason of part-time employment or fixed-term contract. As well as this, employers are bound by law to ensure that procedures are in place for complaints by staff to be pursued. However, a word of caution should be added here: pursuing complaints as an individual could be a difficult, time-consuming and, ultimately, very dispiriting business. To do so without the advice and support of a trade union or professional association is not recommended, even for the most experienced of us.

Special Educational Needs

The world of education has undergone many shifts in the last fifteen or twenty years, but few have been so profound as the way in which we deal with children with Special Educational Needs (SEN). From a position in many schools where a few children were herded off into a separate room under the supervision of 'the remedial teacher', SEN is now at the heart of most schools' practice. A glance at the statutory duties of schools, drawn from the *Code of Practice* last updated in 2001, reinforces this position.

The governing bodies of maintained schools have important statutory duties towards pupils with SEN. The main ones, as outlined by the *TeacherNet* website, are as follows:

- to decide the school's SEN policy and approach, setting up appropriate staffing and funding arrangements and oversee the school's work
- to do its best to ensure that the necessary provision is made for any pupil who has a special need
- to ensure that teachers in the school are aware of the importance of identifying and providing for those pupils who have SEN
- to ensure that a pupil with SEN joins in the activities of the school, together with pupils who do not have SEN, as far as is reasonably practical
- to report to parents on the implementation of the school's policy for pupils with SEN and notify them when SEN provision is being made for their child
- to have regard to the Code of Practice when carrying out duties towards all pupils with SEN
- to appoint a 'responsible person', who makes sure that all those who work with a child with a statement of SEN are told about the statement

IEPs – legal documents?

At the end of a busy day, the last thing you might want to see in your pigeonhole or in-tray is a stack of Individual Education Plans – IEPs. You might grumblingly acknowledge that these are important working documents; it's just that you don't much feel like doing them on top of everything else. In an effort to twist your arm the SENCO might just remind you that IEPs are legal documents. Is he or she correct?

The legal status of the Code, let us remember, is that we must 'have regard' to it. So, if it is the case that your school has decided to meet the needs of SEN children in a way that incorporates the use of IEPs – and this has clearly been made known to you – then in a very roundabout way the SENCO is technically correct by invoking the law in this way. You know that you'll have to do them sooner or later, so I wouldn't advise entering into some great legal wrangle about this!

The 'responsible person' of the last bullet point is usually called the Special Educational Needs Co-ordinator, or SENCO, and it is through this person that most information and necessary documentation is routed. Whilst it is true that it is upon this person that the majority of these obligations will fall, you, as an individual teacher, must also recognise the information and background you have been given about pupils, adjusting your own practice accordingly.

The legal status of the SEN *Code of Practice*, which, like all DfES circulars and publications, is available online, is interesting and illuminating. The penultimate bullet point on p.41 refers to schools having 'regard' to the Code. What this means is that although the implementation of the Code is not, in fact, a legal requirement, schools would have to demonstrate that the provision made to meet the needs of children with SEN is at least as good as the guidance laid down in the Code itself. In other words, schools can devise their own practices but, in reality, few choose to stray from the advice given in the Code, which in its own preface acknowledges that some diversity of approach is necessary:

This Code of Practice is effective from 1 January 2002. From that date LEAs, schools, early education settings and those who help them – including health and social services – must have regard to it. They must not ignore it. That means that whenever settings, schools and LEAs decide how to exercise their functions relating to children with special educational needs, and whenever the health and social services provide help to settings, schools and LEAs in this, those bodies must consider what this Code says. These bodies must fulfil their statutory duties towards children with special educational needs but it is up to them to decide how to do so – in the light of the guidance in this Code of Practice. The Code is designed to help them to make effective decisions but it does not – and could not – tell them what to do in each individual case.

Generally, overall provision for SEN children rests at the level of school management but, depending on your circumstances, you will almost certainly be dealing with SEN issues every day of your working life. It is most unlikely that as a subject or class teacher at the start of your career, anyone will challenge the legality of what you, personally, provide for SEN pupils. (Such challenges, incidentally, almost always come from parents or carers.) It is, however, a matter of contractual obligation on your part to ensure that proper provision is made in your classes for all pupils.

Competence, capability, and disciplinary procedures

To achieve a system whereby we can remove the failing teacher from the classroom, we need speedy but fair procedures. That is clearly not the case under the present arrangements, in which there are at least five separate stages before a teacher can be removed from the classroom. The procedure starts with an informal warning; there is then a formal oral warning, a written warning, a disciplinary hearing and then a final appeal. On average, the process takes eighteen months. That is unacceptable. It is understandable that heads and governing bodies are often reluctant to embark on such a complex and time-consuming process. It simply has to change.

– Stephen Byers, then Minister of State (School Standards),
Department for Education and Employment,
in a Commons answer in July 1997

One can understand the anxiety of anyone, be it a parent, colleague, head teacher or even a minister of state, at the thought of an incompetent teacher in charge of any class. But if ever there was an instance of tilting at windmills, the great fuss over dealing with incompetent teachers really is a case in point. Chris Woodhead, head of OFSTED at the time, claimed that there were some 15,000 incompetent teachers operating in our schools. So what is the truth about this particular problem, and how likely is it that any of this will affect you?

Before we look at the legal position, let us investigate the extent of the problem. Starting with capability, or general competence, University of Manchester research published in 2002 found that, of the total teaching force, only some 1.2 per cent ever reached the point where their performance

Capability or disciplinary?

Sometimes the lines between these two areas are a little blurred, but generally speaking, this rough set of examples should help you to see that there is a difference.

Capability (sometimes called competence) procedures generally stem from the performance of an individual as a class teacher: problematic subject knowledge, failing to mark and assess properly, late completion of reports and, perhaps most frequently, very poor classroom management are the most frequent areas for concern.

Disciplinary procedures, which deal with conduct up to and including gross misconduct, cover areas such as theft and fraud, false claims, discriminatory behaviour, abuse of drugs or alcohol affecting the completion of professional duties, or the deliberate failure to carry out an instruction from the school's managers.

A fuller (and very frightening) list of the sorts of areas covered can be found on the website of the General Teaching Council (see 'Further reading', p.51), which issues its own *Code of Conduct and Practice*.

But remember ... fewer than one in every hundred teachers ever falls foul of such procedures!

gave their managers cause for concern. Only 0.67 per cent reached the point where they had to move to the invoking of actual procedures. Of this 0.67 per cent, ultimately some 50 per cent resigned and around 30 per cent improved. You don't need to be a mathematical genius to calculate that of some 400,000 teachers working in England, there are not the hordes of incompetents conjured up by Woodhead. (0.67 per cent of 400,000 is 2,680, to save you diving for your calculator.) However, the claim that a full investigation along with hearings generally takes around eighteen months is, in fact, borne out by the research.

When it comes to the use of disciplinary proceedings against teachers covering, for example, allegations of misconduct as opposed to incompetence, there is no research similar to that completed in Manchester.

Nevertheless, although such cases are uncommon, many that fall into the category of misconduct – and especially that of gross misconduct – often go beyond the remit of the school's own procedures.

The first thing to take into account is that in the unlikely event of your being on the wrong end of these procedures, unless your misdemeanours mean that you have, in fact, broken the law, their application is in-house and will not involve agencies outside education. The procedures that a school chooses to use are not prescribed by law; they will usually be modelled on advice given by local authorities which, in turn, will have acknowledged advice from the DfES. (In the case of schools of a religious nature, it is likely that the ruling bodies of the religious organisations to which they have affiliation will have made some contribution to the formulation of regulations and policies.)

It simply cannot be emphasised too strongly that the majority of day-to-day disputes or concerns about performance are dealt with on an informal level with matters resolved and with all parties moving on. However, if this does not happen informally, all procedures to be used – and schools must have such procedures by law – need to be open, transparent and fair. Although there are probably hundreds of sets of such procedures, there will only be occasional differences of emphasis between them, and all of them must allow for the following:

- Any teacher accused of failure of competence or of a disciplinary offence must be furnished with a set of the procedures that are to be used at the outset of any proceedings
- Teachers finding themselves in such a position have the right to be accompanied by a friend or trade union representative at every stage of the proceedings
- The procedures must make it clear what the process is in terms of time limits, hearings and potential outcomes
- The right to appeal must be included in all such procedures

Do bear in mind that the terms 'hearings', 'procedures', and 'appeals', as intimidating as they sound, do not mean that these instances are 'tried' in a court of law. Hearings themselves usually take place on school premises, and any judgements are made by members of the school's governing bodies. Although it is just possible in the event of gross misconduct that such hearings may end up in dismissal, a much more common outcome is a warning of some sort along with the establishment of a period of time during which improvements have to be made or issues addressed. It is also part of the school's duty of care to ensure that support is put in place in order to effect such improvements.

The plain fact is that, should you be unfortunate enough to find yourself embroiled in such a situation, you would need to take immediate advice from your trade union or professional association. (Remember the point made earlier: you won't be able to join retrospectively in such circumstances.) Leafing through unfamiliar documents about proceedings and hearings at a time of great stress and uncertainty is the last thing anyone would need to be doing.

What of your conduct outside school? By the time you are first appointed you will have completed an *Enhanced Disclosure* from the Criminal Records Bureau. This will show any acquittals, non-convictions, or convictions that you may have. Failure to complete this honestly, no matter how minor the offence, may well result in disciplinary procedures from the school that could, in turn, lead to dismissal. Once in service, it goes without saying that any criminal offence committed by you will be dealt with by the law in the usual way: but what view will the school take of this, and what actions might your employers take? Obviously, the most significant factor here is the seriousness of the offence itself. The sort of minor indiscretions perpetrated by younger and less experienced teachers outside school are, more often than not, thoughtless episodes of behaviour which usually merit a small fine and a great deal of embarrassment. It is possible that your employer might take a position on this, especially if the misdemeanour has gone into the public domain. The school may simply choose to issue an informal word of warning; but if it chooses instead to pursue the matter and invoke disciplinary procedures, you would need to follow the advice given earlier in this section.

So, to recap …

I hope that the big messages of this guide have now become clear. If not, here is the digested version:

For most teachers in the normal course of events, it is not necessary to know a great deal about the law and how it affects you, although knowing the precise nature of what is meant by 'duty of care' along with your contractual obligations is very important.

The number of teachers who fall foul of the law when conducting their professional duties is almost statistically insignificant.

Acquainting yourself with the policies and procedures in your particular school, and applying these consistently, is easily the best way of protecting yourself against accusations of negligence or abuse.

Joining a trade union or professional association is vital. Joining your subject association is also highly recommended.

I would be surprised if some trainee teachers or others new to the profession were not just a touch sceptical about some of the points made in the guide. What if, for example, there are no policies about behaviour, health and safety, physical restraint, or any of the other areas we've touched on, readily available in the school? And do you, as a new and inexperienced member of staff, really want to draw attention to yourself by asking to see such documents if they're not easily to be found? Might it seem a little strange if, on your first day, you were to ask to know who was the lead professional for child protection? Are you ready to be the first one to point out that parental consent to detention is not required, or that in loco parentis is an outdated and fairly useless concept?

There are no glib answers here, but there are a few things that you might want to consider. The first of these would be to try to ascertain at interview whether there are basic behaviour management policies in place and, most importantly, whether there are arrangements made for the induction of new staff where questions about policies will be dealt with and key personnel will be identified. (Incidentally, an induction programme is an entitlement for teachers in their NQT year, although there are no stipulations about the form that this should take.) The sort of answers you receive to these enquiries may well be instrumental in reaching a decision about whether that particular school is for you.

There is an ongoing joke amongst those of us who have made teacher trade unionism part of our lives about how we got ourselves involved. It starts with a simple question at a staff meeting about why the heating is so temperamental or whether refreshments can be provided on those evenings when staff need to stay late, and it ends with you being the school union representative and, most likely, a place on your local union committee. Although there is a deal of folklore about trade union membership being a barrier to promotion and advancement, there is not much evidence to support this. The law is absolutely unequivocal in ensuring that membership of a trade union and promoting trade-union activities as a representative or an officer cannot be used as reasons for discriminating against a teacher in matters of employment, promotion, redundancy or dismissal. The *Employment Rights Act 1996* enshrines these rights in law. What is more, there is plenty of evidence to show that a willingness to engage with such issues often goes hand in glove with a clear understanding of the major educational issues of the day: and that can be a real advantage when going for promoted posts. True professionalism is about knowing how the law works for you – and even helping to frame it – as well as recognising how it works for our pupils.

> Sometimes I think that staff don't talk up enough. It's no use something happening and then bringing it up weeks later.
>
> – Secondary school teacher

Further reading

In putting together this section I am working on the assumption that someone about to embark upon a career teaching the nation's children knows how to use a simple search engine. As a consequence, I have only listed those sites that I consider to be the most important, and to which I expect you may wish to refer most frequently. In the event of your needing to locate something a little more specialised or obscure, I am sure that some judicious searching will yield what you need.

TeacherNet at www.teachernet.gov.uk is a thorough and comprehensive site that gives links and access to a wide range of policies, advice, and documentation, as does the Training Development Agency for Schools' site at www.tda.gov.uk.

The website of the National Union of Teachers at www.nut.org.uk gives advice, information, and contacts for a wide range of issues affecting teachers, including who to contact in times of difficulty. The websites of other teacher organisations may offer similar services.

The Department for Education and Skills at www.dfes.gov.uk operates an extensive website, the search facility taking you quickly to all the main subject areas such as behaviour management, school trips, and most of the issues covered in this guide.

If you are interested in the Every Child Matters initiative, the website at www.everychildmatters.gov.uk will be useful for you.

As all teachers in England need to be a member of the General Teaching Council, and as this is a statutory body which regulates the profession, you may wish to look at their website: www.gtce.org.uk

As far as all of the principal legislation referred to in this guide is concerned, simply typing the name into any search engine – *Race Relations*

(Amendment) Act, Disability Discrimination Act, Health and Safety at Work Act, and so on – will generate not only copies of legislation itself, but also information on practical applications of the law.